Recorder from the Beginning
Tune Book 1

Thirty-six Solos and Seven Duets to Complement
Recorder from the Beginning Book 1

John Pitts

Introduction

Recorder from the Beginning Tune Books 1, 2 and 3 provide material to supplement the author's teaching scheme *Recorder from the Beginning* Books 1, 2 and 3. This teaching scheme assumes no previous knowledge of either music or the recorder and provides full explanations at every stage. However, some children need more practice material than others to consolidate their skills at particular stages. Conversely, some pupils learn quickly and need extra material to hold their interest while the rest of the group catch up. The Tune Books provide for either situation, depending on individual needs.

All the material is carefully graded, following the order of progression in the teaching scheme. However, in keeping with the "repertoire" nature of these supplementary books, very little teaching help or explanation is given. Where such help is required it is best to refer to the appropriate pages of the teaching scheme. Cross-references are provided for this purpose.

Acknowledgements

The publishers would like to thank the following for permission to include their copyright material: Jan Holdstock, the words to "Tiger"; Spike Milligan, the words to "Tell Me, Little Woodworm" and "Hello, Mister Python".

The music on the following pages has been specially composed and arranged by the author: 4, 5, 6, 7, 8 (top); 9, 10 (top); 11, 14, 15 (top); 18, 19, 20 (top); 21 (top); 25, 29, 31.

Contents

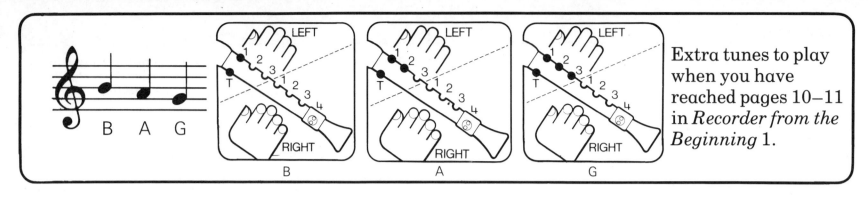

Extra tunes to play when you have reached pages 10–11 in *Recorder from the Beginning* 1.

Rain, Rain

Rain, rain, go a—way. Come a—gain an—oth—er day.

Tiger

Words by Jan Holdstock

Ti—ger, I've a friend with me. Can you give us both a ride?

Yes, boy, cer—tain—ly. One on top and one in—side!

Sua-gan (Welsh)

New note: ♩
See *Recorder from the Beginning* 1, pages 12–14.

Zoogie

Ze —— bra,   ti —— ger,   kan — ga — roo,   snake,

Pen —— guins,   po — lar bears   swim — ming in the lake.

Merrily We Roll Along

Au Claire de la Lune

(Repeat)

5

Lockwood Dance

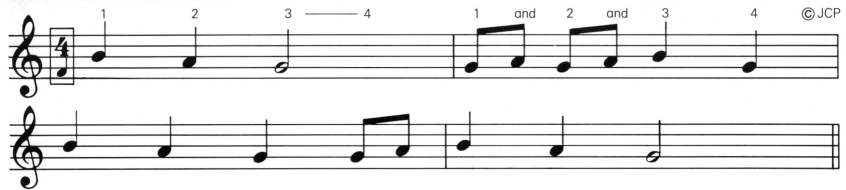

© JCP

New sign: 𝄽
See *Recorder from the Beginning* 1, page 15.

Kangaroos

© JCP

Look at the Bear

Dotted note: ♩.
See *Recorder from the Beginning* 1, pages 16–17.

© JCP

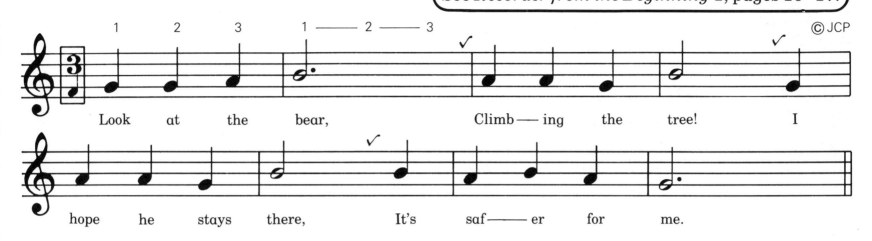

Look   at   the   bear,   Climb — ing   the   tree!   I

hope   he   stays   there,   It's   saf —— er   for   me.

Ask a friend to add an accompaniment on tambourine.
Here is a repeating pattern (ostinato) to use.
It will fit *either* tune on this page.

(1) 2 3   (1) 2 3

✓ means "take a breath".
See *Recorder from the Beginning* 1, page 17.

Leodian Waltz

© JCP

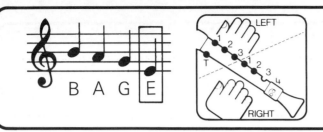

New note: E.
See *Recorder from the Beginning* 1, pages 18–19.

Old Sammy Snail

© JCP

Old Sam - my Snail, he crawls down the leaf. He

takes his time 'cause he has — n't an — y feet.

When you can play **Old Sammy Snail**, ask a friend to accompany you.
Your friend plays the last bar ("feet") again and again as an ostinato
while you play the tune. Then you can swap over.

It's Raining   Count 1–2–3 then play on count 4.

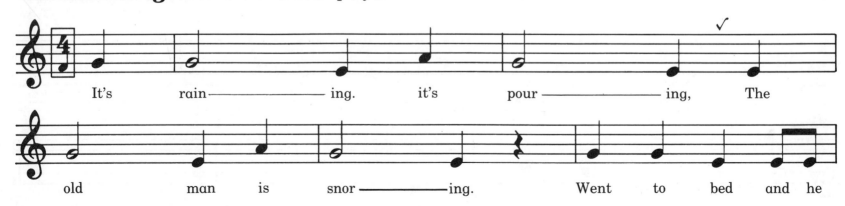

It's rain———————ing. it's pour———————ing, The

old man is snor———————ing. Went to bed and he

8

It's Raining (continued)

bumped his head, And he did—n't get up in the mor———ning.

Rigi River

Tied notes: See *Recorder from the Beginning 1*, pages 20–21.

*Lines 2 and 4 are the same!

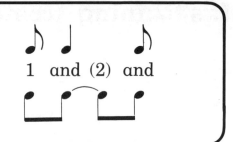

Falsgrave March

© JCP

Chinese Folk-song

Tell Me, Little Woodworm

Words by Spike Milligan

New note: See *Recorder from the Beginning* 1, page 22.

Tell me, lit—tle wood———worm, Eat—ing through the wood,

Sure—ly all that saw—dust Can't do you an—y good.

Heav—ens, lit—tle wood———worm, You've eat—en all the chairs! So

that's why poor old Gran—dad's Sit—ting out—side on the stairs!

When you can play the tune well, ask a friend to accompany you by playing this ostinato. Use the largest (lowest-sounding) xylophone you have.

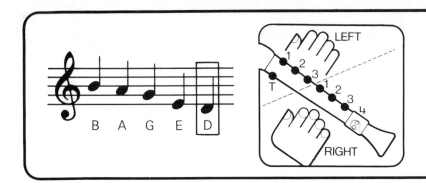

New note: D.
See *Recorder from the Beginning 1*, pages 24–25.

Tom Dooley

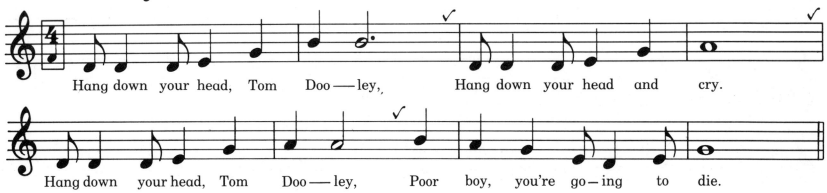

Hang down your head, Tom Doo — ley, Hang down your head and cry.

Hang down your head, Tom Doo — ley, Poor boy, you're go — ing to die.

Ask some friends to play an accompaniment to **Tom Dooley**. They can use any of the ostinati below. Each pattern may be played either by itself or with the others. Use a different instrument for each ostinato: for example, a xylophone, metallophone and glockenspiel.

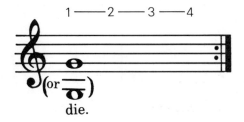

(or 𝅝) die.

Hang down your head, Tom

Doo — ley.

Old Brass Wagon

For the rhythm ♩ ♫ see *Recorder from the Beginning* 1, page 24.

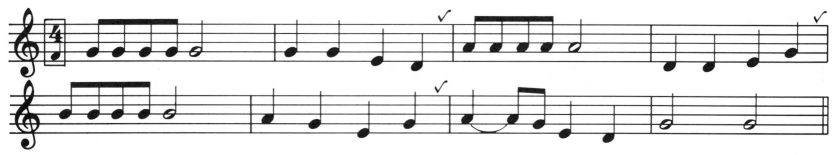

For the rhythm ♫ ♩ see *Recorder from the Beginning* 1, page 22.

The Gospel Train   Count 1–2 then play on count 3.

The gos——pel train's a ——com——ing, I hear it just at hand,—— I hear the car wheels rum—bling, And rol—ling through the land. Get on—— board, lit-tle chil—dren, Get on—— board, lit-tle chil-dren, Get on—— board, lit-tle chil-dren, There's room for ma-ny a more.

Macugnaga Waltz

For **slurring**, see *Recorder from the Beginning 1*, pages 26–27.

© JCP

Zilina Polka

For **staccato notes**, see *Recorder from the Beginning 1*, pages 30–31.

© JCP

Zilina Polka (continued)

Old Time Religion (Spiritual) Count 1–2 then play on count 3.

Give me that old time ___ re-li—gion, Give me that old time ___ re-

li—gion, Give me that old time ___ re-li—gion, It's good e———nough for me.

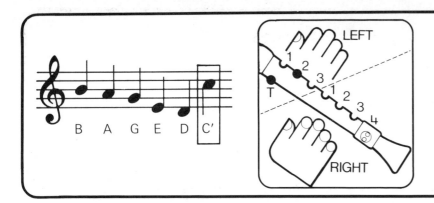

New note: C'
See *Recorder from the Beginning 1*,
pages 32–33.

Rigadoon by Purcell

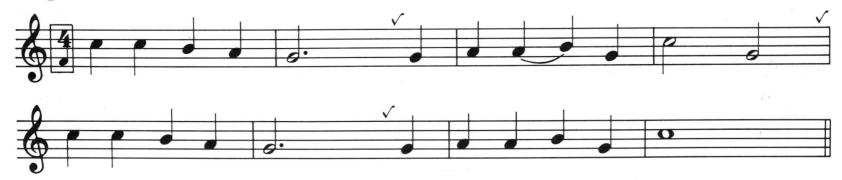

Pease Pudding Hot

16

Israeli Folk-song

Sur le Pont de Nantes   Count 1–2 then play on count 3.

Punta di Crabbia

When you can play this tune, try the descant.
It begins with the same music.
Later, you and a friend could play both tunes together.

© JCP

Brozany Polka

© JCP

Fine

Descant to Punta di Crabbia

Fine means "end".
Da Capo means "go back to the beginning".

Glen Garry   Count 1–2 then play on count 3.

Never Sleep Late Any More   Count 1–2–3 then play on count 4.

Oh,   just   let   me   get   up   in   the   ear——ly   morn,

Just   let   me   get   up   in   the   ear—ly   morn,   Just   let   me   get   up   in   the

Descant to Glen Garry

Count 1–2 then play on count 3.

© JCP

ear———ly   morn   And I'll nev—er   sleep late   an—y   more.

The Bells of Vendôme

Cobbler's Jig

See *Recorder from the Beginning* 1, pages 34–35.

Les Bouffons (French)

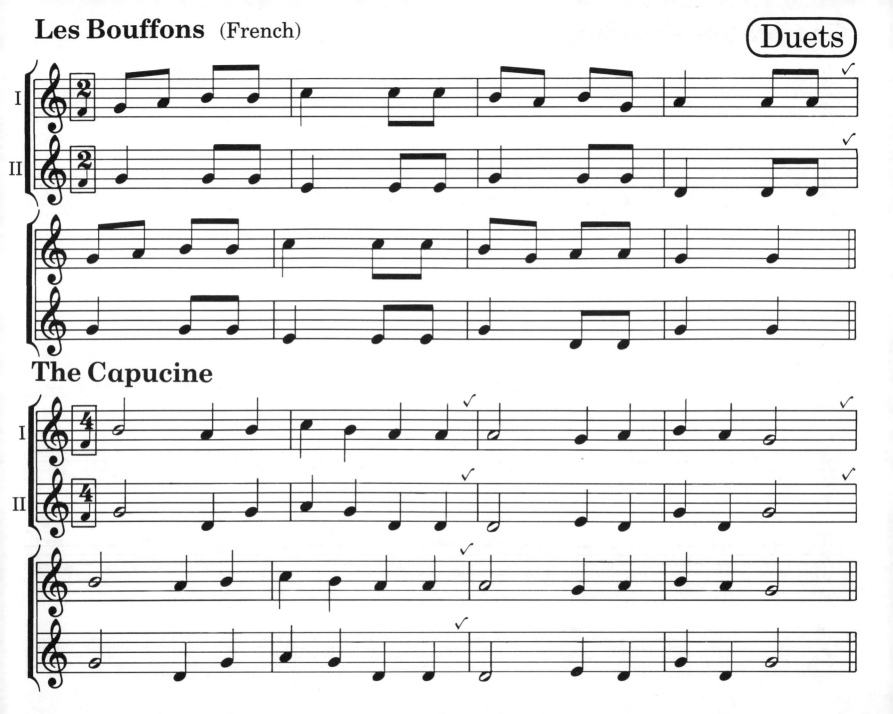

Duets

The Capucine

23

Go from My Window

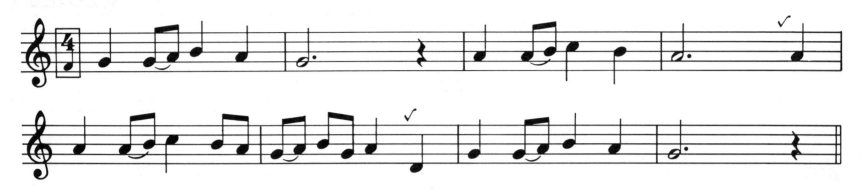

The Grand Old Duke of York Count 1–2 then play on count 3.

Gemsstock

Fine means "end".
Da Capo means "go back to the beginning".

Duet

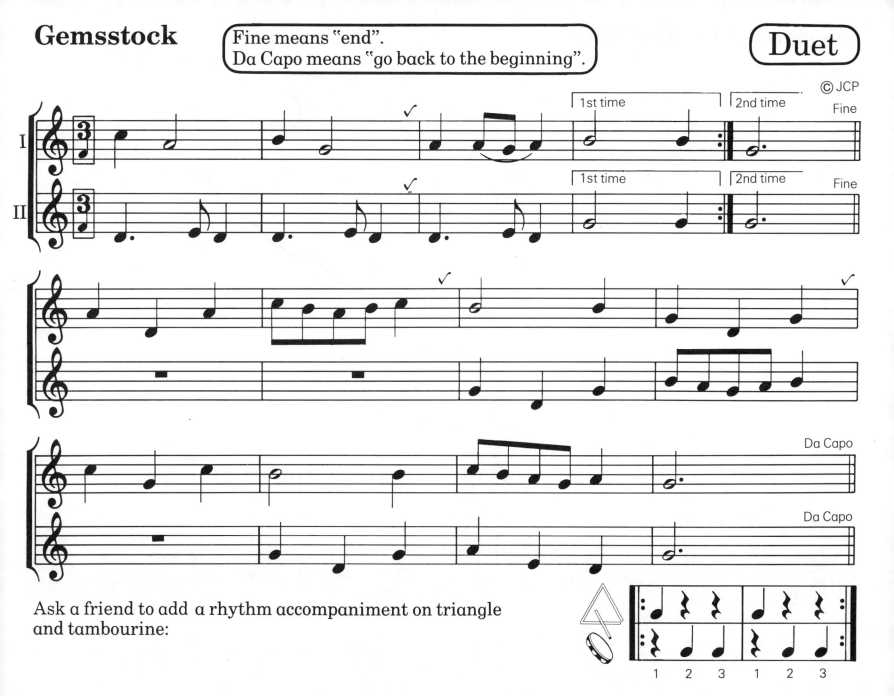

Ask a friend to add a rhythm accompaniment on triangle and tambourine:

Down in the Meadow

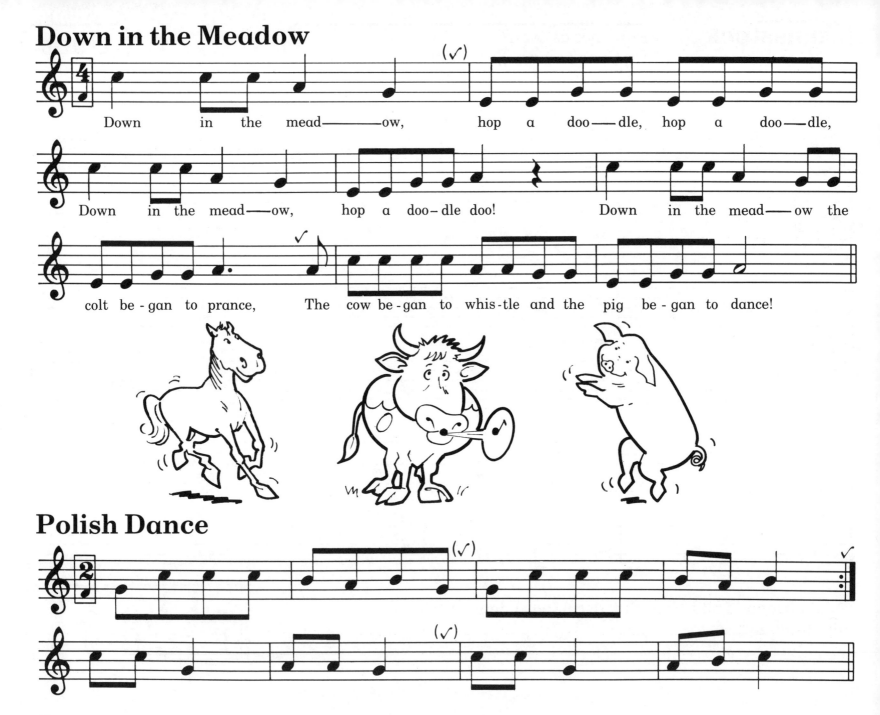

Down in the mead——ow, hop a doo—dle, hop a doo—dle,

Down in the mead——ow, hop a doo-dle doo! Down in the mead——ow the

colt be-gan to prance, The cow be-gan to whis-tle and the pig be-gan to dance!

Polish Dance

Duet

French Folk-song Count 1–2 then play on count 3.

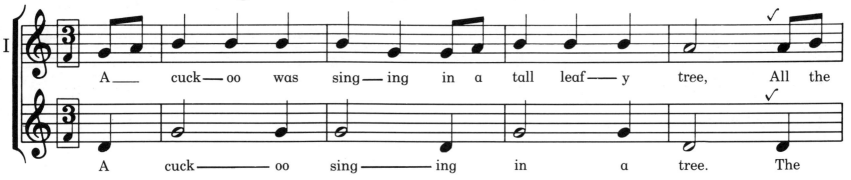

A cuck—oo was sing—ing in a tall leaf—y tree, All the

A cuck——oo sing——ing in a tree. The

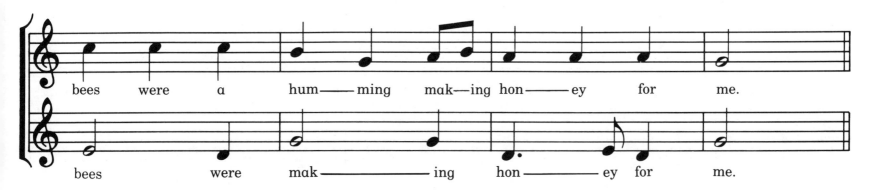

bees were a hum——ming mak—ing hon——ey for me.

bees were mak——ing hon——ey for me.

Volga Boatman's Song

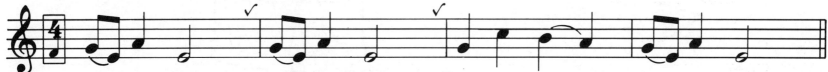

Aiken Drum

Count 1–2–3 then play on count 4.

There lived a man in our town, in our town, in our town, There lived a man in our town, His name was Ai —ken Drum. And he would be a sol —dier, a sol —dier, a sol —dier, And he would be a sol —dier, And his name was Ai —ken Drum.

28

Duet

Chandos Fanfare

Player I counts 1–2–3 then plays on count 4.

Player II counts 1–2–3–4   1–2–3 then plays on count 4.

© JCP

29

Making up tunes using notes we know

D E (F) G A B C'

Try pages 38–39 in *Recorder from the Beginning 1* **before** you start this page.

See if you can make up some music to finish off the tune on the next page. Follow the instructions carefully.

A   Say and clap line 1, then play it.

B   Make up an ending for line 2. First play the beginning that is given. Then say and clap the words of the rest of the line. Now make up a tune to fit the words you clapped.

      Use any of the notes you know. Keep trying until you like your tune. Make sure it fits the rest of the tune. Then write it down.

C   Finish line 3 in the same way. Say and clap the words first. Keep trying different notes to fill the spaces until you like the tune. Then write down the notes.

D   Finish line 4 in the same way. Now play the whole tune.

30

Hello, Mister Python

Words by Spike Milligan

A: Hel—lo, Mis—ter Py—thon, Cur—ling round a tree,

B: Bet you'd like to make your—self A din—ner out of me!

C: Can't you change your hab—its Crush—ing peo—ple's bones? I

D: would-n't like a din—ner That e—mit—ted fear—ful groans!

Fingering Chart
English (Baroque) Fingered Recorders

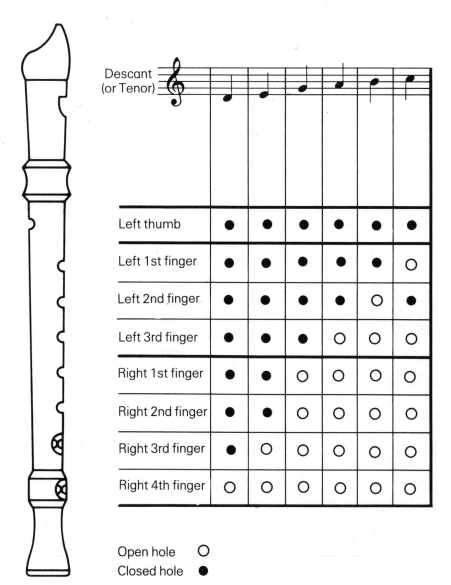

Descant (or Tenor)						
Left thumb	●	●	●	●	●	●
Left 1st finger	●	●	●	●	●	○
Left 2nd finger	●	●	●	●	○	●
Left 3rd finger	●	●	●	○	○	○
Right 1st finger	●	●	○	○	○	○
Right 2nd finger	●	●	○	○	○	○
Right 3rd finger	●	○	○	○	○	○
Right 4th finger	○	○	○	○	○	○

Open hole ○
Closed hole ●

Printed and bound in Great Britain by Caligraving Limited Thetford Norfolk